Adam's New Friend
and Other Stories from the Bible

David and Carol Bartlett
Illustrated by Scott Stapleton

Judson Press ® Valley Forge

Adam's New Friend and Other Stories from the Bible
Copyright © 1980
Judson Press, Valley Forge, PA 19481

Library of Congress Cataloging in Publication Data

Bartlett, David.
  Adam's new friend, and other stories from the Bible.

  SUMMARY: Retellings of familiar Bible stories especially for the young.
  1. Bible stories, English. (1. Bible stories) I. Bartlett, Carol, joint author.
II. Stapleton, Scott. III. Title.
BS551.2.B36   220.9'505   80-279
ISBN 0-8170-0882-9

The name JUDSON PRESS is registered as a trademark in the U.S. Patent Office.
Printed in the U.S.A. ⊕

*For Madeleine Stapleton and for
Benjamin Bartlett and Jonah Bartlett*

Contents

Introduction

These stories are written to be told or read aloud. The style suggests story telling rather than book reading. When told, the stories need not be memorized word for word. Often they contain devices like repetition to help the teller remember the movement and the key points of the tale.

Most of these stories have been told aloud to children, often during the Sunday morning worship service. We hope they will also find a place in church school and at home. The reader of the stories will note that some of them are appropriate especially for younger children, some for older.

Our hope is that the stories present to children some of the great stories of the Bible, with something of the seriousness and something of the humor of the originals. Their purpose is not so much to point a moral as to open the world of the Bible, so that children may learn to love the stories and delight in the biblical faith.

We are especially grateful to those children who have heard many of these stories and who in not so subtle ways have helped us to tell them more effectively. We appreciate the editorial suggestions of Harold Twiss and Cynthia Mooney at Judson Press. And we express our heartfelt thanks to the people of Hyde Park Union Church in Chicago who encouraged us to write and draw this book.

Adam's New Friend

Once upon a time (so the story goes), God decided to make something good and delightful.

So God took some dirt and spat upon the dirt, and the dirt turned into clay. Then God molded the clay (as you might mold clay) into a doll shaped like a man. Then God breathed into the doll, and the doll became a living, breathing human being. Indeed, it became the very first living, breathing human being. God said, "Your name is Adam." In those days, in the language in which God was speaking, *Adam* meant "man."

Now Adam looked around at the world, and the world was very lovely. Green grass. Blue skies. Trees dripping with fruit. Streams. Lakes. You name it; Adam had it.

But something was missing. Adam thought a long time about what was missing, and then he spoke to God and said, "I'm lonely. I need someone to be my friend, to help me get along."

"No sooner said than done," said God. "Look!"

God pointed to the lakes and streams, and Adam bent over to look into the nearest stream. There were fish of all sizes swimming about—minnows and mackerels, pike and pickerel, catfish and carp. "Nice," said Adam. "Fun to watch and fun to catch but not exactly what I had in mind. Do you think that you could make something a little more, well—beautiful?"

"No sooner said than done," said God. "Look!"

God pointed to the sky, and Adam looked up to see the sky filled with birds. Birds flew through the air and rested in the trees: bluebirds and redbirds, birds with plumes and birds with tails like fans. The world was filled with the songs of birds: some low and gentle, some high and sharp.

"Lovely," said Adam. "Lovely to look at and lovely to listen to but not exactly what I had in mind. Do you think you could make something a little, well—warmer?"

"No sooner said than done," said God. "Look!"

God pointed to the forests and fields. Adam looked and saw that the forests and fields were full of animals. Large furry animals with claws and small fuzzy animals with bright eyes and long tails. Animals that went, "Grr!" Animals that went, "Moo."

Adam was impressed. "I'm impressed," said Adam. "So many different kinds of animals. And so useful, too, I might guess. But still not exactly what I had in mind. Do you think you could make something a little more—how shall I say it?—a little more like *me*?"

"Too much like you would be boring," said God.

"A good point," said Adam. "How about something different enough to be interesting but like enough to be friendly?"

"Ah," said God, "you don't want me to make some*thing.* You want me to make some*one.*"

"Yes," said Adam. "That's it. That's what I want."

"That's a little harder," said God. "Close your eyes."

Adam closed his eyes and seemed to doze for a while. "Open your eyes," said God.

Adam opened his eyes. He saw someone who was different enough to be interesting and like enough to be friendly.

"What is it?" asked Adam.

"You mean, 'Who is it?'" said God.

"All right, *who* is it?"

"She is a woman," said God. "Her name is Eve."

"That's more like it," said Adam. Then he turned to the woman. "How do you do?"

(Based on Genesis 2:18-25)

11

Names

One of the most important gifts your parents gave you was your name. Even before you were born, they thought and thought, wondering what they were going to name you.

Perhaps they chose your name because they liked the sound of it. Perhaps they named you after a special friend or relative. Perhaps they named you after someone in the Bible or some other famous person. Perhaps they named you because your name means something nice.

When your parents chose your name, they showed that even though you are a gift from God, you also belong to them in a special way. They share in caring for you, loving you, guiding you.

Now once upon a time, as we already saw, the story says that God made the first man and the first woman. God also made fish and birds, flowers, trees, and animals.

After the first man (named Adam) and the first woman (named Eve) had had a chance to get acquainted, God showed them all the world which God had made.

"Look!" said God. God pointed to the streams, then to the skies, then to the earth. Streams, skies, and earth were full of green things growing, silvery things swimming, feathered things flying, and brown things

running all over the ground and saying, "Grr!"

Eve pointed to one of the brown things running about saying, "Grr!"

"What's that?" asked Eve.

"You tell me," said God.

"How should I know?" said Eve. "I just got here, and I've never seen one of those things before."

"*You* name it," said God. "You and Adam can decide what that is going to be called."

Adam looked hard at the brown thing running around saying, "Grr!"

"Let's call it a 'brown, growling runabout,'" said Adam.

"That's a little long," said Eve. "How about something shorter like 'qrwksk'?"

"Qrwksk!?" said Adam. "That's too hard to say—'Look at the qrwksk!'—it won't do."

"I've got it," said Eve. "Let's call it a 'bear.'"

"Bear," said Adam. "I like that. All right, brown thing running around saying 'Grr!', we name you 'Bear.'"

"Good," said God. "Now go on."

"Go on?" asked Eve.

"Yes, go on. Name them all. The green things growing, the silvery things swimming, the feathered things flying, the furry things bustling about. You name them all."

"Why us?" asked Adam.

"Because that way all those things will belong to you as well as to me," said God. "That way you'll know that they're yours to care for and watch over and protect."

"That sounds like fun," said Adam. "Come on, Eve,

let's try again. Look at that! Let's call it a red-breasted, brown-winged, flying, chirping worm-eater. What do you think, Eve?"

"Adam, Adam," said Eve, "this could take a long time."

(Based on Genesis 1:26-31; 2:18-19)

Noah

God looked around and saw that the people on earth had forgotten that God had created them—had created them, named them, and cared for them. They had forgotten that God had told them to name and care for all the living creatures on earth. All of these things deeply saddened God, and so God decided to send a great flood which would cover all the earth.

However, just about the time that God had decided to send this flood, God saw that a man named Noah and all of Noah's family had not forgotten God. They remembered that God created them and cared for them. They remembered that they were to care for all of God's creatures. This pleased God. God decided that since Noah and his family had remembered God and cared for God's creation, God would remember them.

God said to Noah: "Noah, I want you to make an ark [that's God's word for a ship] out of gopher wood. I want you to make an ark with many rooms and cover it inside and out with pitch so it will stay afloat."

"OK, God," Noah said, "but I have to tell you I've never made an ark before. In fact, I don't even know what an ark is!"

"Don't worry, Noah," God said. "I will tell you how to make it. The ark should be three hundred cubits long, fifty cubits wide, and thirty cubits high. It should be three stories high and have a roof."

"God," Noah said, "I want to thank you for all this help, but we have a nice little house here. It's really big enough for us. I'm not sure we need a new house and especially a house that floats."

"Noah," God said, "did I forget to mention to you that I'm sending a flood to cover the earth?"

"Oh," said Noah.

"Now," God said, "I want you to make this ark so that you and your family will be safe when the rain comes."

So Noah and his family built the ark as God had told them, for Noah did all that God commanded him.

"It's finished, God," Noah said, "but I was wondering—are you sure that we need such a big ark? I mean three stories is a lot of room for eight people."

"Noah," said God, "did I forget to mention to you that I want you to gather up two creatures, a girl and a boy, of all the creatures you can find and bring them into the ark?"

"Oh," said Noah.

So Noah and his family went out and gathered up two creatures (a girl and a boy) of all the creatures they could find—beastly creatures, creeping creatures, crawling creatures, and flying creatures—and brought them into the ark, for Noah did all that God commanded him.

The heavens opened up, and the rain began to fall. It rained and rained for forty days and forty nights, covering the earth completely. The ark floated for days and days, 150 to be exact, and Noah and his family were beginning to wonder if God had forgotten them.

"I have an idea," said Noah. "I'll send out a dove, and

18

if the dove finds a place to land and food to eat, we will know that God has not forgotten us. We will know that the waters are going down." So Noah opened the window of the ark and let a dove fly away.

Later that evening the dove returned with a freshly plucked olive leaf in its beak. Noah now knew that God had not forgotten them and that the waters were drying up from the earth.

God came to Noah and his family and said, "Noah, it is time for you to leave the ark and to begin again."

Noah and his family were very thankful to God, and to show their thanks, they built an altar and presented gifts to God. This so pleased God that God promised Noah that God would always care for Noah, his children, and his children's children forever.

"Noah," God said, "as a sign of my love and caring for you and all of my creation, I will put a rainbow in the sky, and when I look at the rainbow, I will remember my promise to care for you always."

(Based on Genesis 6:11–9:17)

The Story of Joseph, I
Joseph and His Coat

Many of you have brothers and sisters, and you know how it goes. You love them, but sometimes you think that they get more than their share. They get more allowance than you. Or they get to stay up later than you. Or you think that your brother's new sweater is nicer than your new sweater, or your sister's new dress is nicer than your new dress—if you have a sister and wear dresses.

The Bible tells a story about a family of brothers. There were twelve of them. I won't tell you all their names. One of them was named Joseph, and his older brothers were jealous of Joseph because they thought that he got all kinds of special favors. And while your parents are careful *not* to treat you better or worse than your brothers and sisters, in Joseph's case it didn't work that way. His father really *did* give him special favors; so his brothers had some reason to be upset.

Joseph's brothers had special reason to be upset one day when Joseph's father gave Joseph a present. It was a coat with long sleeves, VERY LONG SLEEVES, sleeves so long that Joseph's fingertips barely showed beyond the cuffs.

Now if you saw a coat so big that the owner's fingertips barely showed at the cuffs, you'd say, "That coat is too big!" But when Joseph's brothers saw the coat, they said, "Lucky Joseph! It's happened again."

They said, "Lucky Joseph!" because they knew that no one who had a coat with long sleeves had to work in the fields. The person who had long sleeves could barely get his fingers, much less his hands and arms and elbows, out of the coat to do the dirty work. So Joseph's brothers knew there would be no more dirty work for Joseph and all the more dirty work for them. They were very angry.

They were so angry that they decided to get rid of Joseph. That sounds terrible, and it *was* terrible. Most of the brothers wanted to kill Joseph, but one of them,

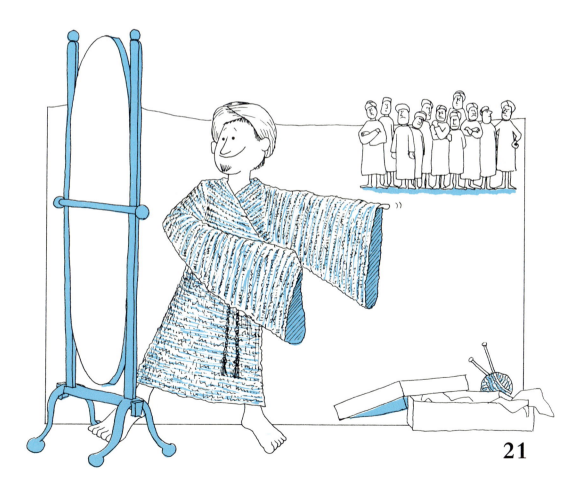

named Reuben, persuaded them to put Joseph in a big hole instead and leave him there. (Secretly Reuben was planning to come back and rescue Joseph and help him escape.)

Joseph didn't know that Reuben planned to come back and help him escape. All he knew was that his brothers came up and grabbed him and threw him into the hole. He was very unhappy. "This is the pits," he said when he found himself at the bottom of a very deep hole.

"How am I going to get out?" he wondered. "Help!" he yelled. Then he was quiet for a very long time. Then he yelled, "Help!" again.

Just then a group of slave traders came marching past. Slave traders were people who sold other people to strangers. The strangers were called masters. The people who got sold were called slaves. Masters could order slaves around.

Being a slave wasn't very nice, but it may have been better than being dead. At least, Joseph's brother Judah thought that being a slave was better than being dead. He said to his brothers, "Let's not leave Joseph to die in the pit. Let's sell him to the slave traders."

So Joseph's brothers had pity on Joseph in the pit. Also, they wanted to make a little money. They pulled him up out of the pit. They sold him to the slave traders.

"Well," thought Joseph, "at least I'm still alive." He went off with the slave traders to find a master who would buy him.

(Based on Genesis 37)

The Story of Joseph, II
Joseph in Egypt

Joseph was very fortunate, if you can ever say a slave is fortunate. As it turned out, the slave traders took Joseph to Egypt. The master who bought Joseph was called Pharaoh. "Pharaoh" was what the Egyptians called their king in those days.

Because Joseph was very clever and because God was with Joseph, Joseph became a very important man. In fact, he was Pharaoh's right-hand man, a kind of vice-Pharaoh.

Meanwhile, back in Canaan, the land where Joseph had come from, Joseph's father and brothers were in trouble. There hadn't been much rain in Canaan, and because there was no rain, they couldn't grow any crops; and because they couldn't grow crops, they were running out of food.

Now Joseph's father had heard that there was food in Egypt; so he took his savings, and he sent Joseph's brothers to Egypt to buy some food. (Of course, Joseph's father and brothers had no idea that Joseph was still alive, much less Pharaoh's right-hand man.)

Joseph's father kept his youngest son, Benjamin, at home because Joseph's father loved Benjamin very much, and he wanted some company.

Off the brothers went to Egypt, and they came to Pharaoh's court. "We need to buy some food, if you please," they said. They were taken immediately to the

24

man in charge of food—their brother Joseph! Joseph recognized them at once, but they didn't recognize him because it had been many years since they'd seen him, because he'd grown up in the meantime, and because he was dressed up like an Egyptian.

Joseph was very excited when he saw his brothers. "How's your father?" he asked. "Fine," they said. "How's your youngest brother, Benjamin?" he asked. "Fine," they said.

Now you'd think that Joseph's brothers would have begun to get suspicious when Joseph asked about their father and about Benjamin, but they were so nervous and worried about getting food that they didn't notice the strange questions.

What was Joseph going to do? Here were his brothers. Some of them had wanted to kill him. All of them had sold him to the slave traders. Should Joseph refuse to give them food? Should Joseph tell them who he was and have them all arrested?

That's not what Joseph did. He gave them the food; he took their money, and he sneakily put the money back in their packs so that they wouldn't really have to pay for the food. Then he told them, "Next time you come, bring your brother Benjamin."

Since Joseph's brothers didn't think there would *be* a next time, they didn't give his request a second thought. They went home and took the food to their father. When they opened their packs, they were amazed to discover that they still had their money, too.

(Based on Genesis 41:37–42:38)

The Story of Joseph, III
The End of the Story

After Joseph's brothers had been back in the land of Canaan, their home, for about a year, they ran out of food again. Still there had been no rain in the land; so there were no crops, and there was nothing to eat.

Again Joseph's father asked Joseph's brothers to go to Egypt where there was lots of food and where, somehow, even after you bought food, you got your money back as well.

Joseph's brothers hemmed and hawed.

"Why are you hemming and hawing?" asked Joseph's father.

Reuben spoke: "Pharaoh's right-hand man told us that if we ever came back, we were to bring Benjamin with us. Of course, we thought we'd never come back; so we didn't pay much attention. Now, if we return, we've got to take Benjamin with us."

"Oh, no!" cried Joseph's father.

"Oh, yes!" cried Joseph's brothers.

Joseph's father thought a long, long time. Then he said: "All right, then. If you must, you must. But if you don't bring Benjamin home safe and sound, it will probably kill me."

The brothers didn't feel very good about that, but what could they do? So off they went to Egypt, all of Joseph's brothers including Benjamin. They came to Pharaoh's court. "We need to buy some more food, if

26

you please," Joseph's brothers said politely.

Again they were taken to see the man in charge of food—their brother Joseph. When Joseph saw Benjamin, he was so excited that he wanted to cry for joy.

But he didn't say, "Hello, I'm Joseph." Instead, he listened to the brothers' request for food. Then he said, "All right."

He told his brothers to get a good night's sleep while his servants bundled up the food for them. When his servants were bundling up the food, Joseph took his own favorite silver cup. He put the cup in one of Benjamin's bags, and then he closed the bag. (You may think this was a little sneaky, and indeed it was.)

When Joseph's brothers got up the next morning, they took their bags of food. They said, "Thank you very much," and they started off toward home.

They hadn't gotten very far before the Egyptian police came running up after them. "You're under arrest," said the police.

"You must be kidding," said Joseph's brothers. "What have we done?"

"Someone stole the vice-Pharaoh's silver cup," said the police, "and we think it was one of you."

"You must be kidding," said Joseph's brothers, but the police began to search their baggage. Finally the police came to Benjamin's pack. They opened the pack and pulled out the silver cup. Benjamin's brothers all looked at him. "You must be kidding," they said.

"I didn't do it," said Benjamin. "I've been framed."

The police told Joseph's brothers that they were all under arrest, and they marched them back to Joseph.

Now Joseph had them! You might think that now at

28

last Joseph was going to put his brothers in jail, and it would have served them right. You'd think that at least Joseph would tell his brothers who he was.

Instead, Joseph said, "Well, the rest of you can take your food and go home. But since the cup was in Benjamin's pack, Benjamin must stay with me."

Joseph's brothers began to hem and haw. "Why are you hemming and hawing?" asked Joseph.

"Our father said that if we didn't bring Benjamin home, it would probably kill him," said Joseph's brothers. "Please don't make us leave Benjamin with you."

Then Joseph had finally had all the suspense he could stand. "Guess what?" he said. "I'm your brother Joseph."

"You've got to be kidding," said his brothers.

Well, you can imagine that the brothers were more than a little nervous about Joseph's being Joseph. Here he was, the brother they had wronged. And he had the power to punish them.

"Forgive us," they said very softly.

"I do," said Joseph.

"Whew!" said Joseph's brothers, greatly relieved.

Then Benjamin stayed with Joseph while Joseph's brothers went home to get their father. They packed up all their goods and left Canaan and came to live with Joseph because he was their long-lost brother, and he also had charge of a lot of food.

(Based on Genesis 43–45)

Slaves

Sometimes we like to tell a story just because it's a good story. But sometimes we like to tell a story because it's an important story; it tells us something about who we are, about the things which matter to us.

Whenever the Jewish people get together for a celebration, they tell a story; for them it is the most important story in the world. It is the story of how they got their freedom.

You see, long ago the people of Israel had been captured by the Egyptians, and the Egyptians had made them slaves. You know what slaves are. Slaves are people whom other people own. Slaves have no freedom. Other people are always telling them what they have to do. Slaves can't make their own plans or live their own lives the way they want to live them. Slavery is pretty awful.

Even God knows slavery is pretty awful. Or maybe *especially* God knows slavery is pretty awful. So God picked a man named Moses and said, "Go down, Moses, to Egypt and tell Pharaoh [which was what they called the king and chief slaveholder], 'Let my people go!'"

Moses said, "Who, me? I'm not much of a speaker."

"You don't have to say much," said God. "Just say, 'Let my people go.'"

Moses marched right up to Pharaoh's palace. "Thus says the Lord," he said, "'Let my people go!'"

30

"No dice," said Pharaoh.

Then God told Moses how to do a number of remarkable things, such as turning the river Nile into blood, producing a huge number of frogs, turning the dust into a pile of worms, and so forth.

Pharaoh was very impressed. "Let my people go," said Moses.

"I'm not *that* impressed," said Pharaoh. "No dice."

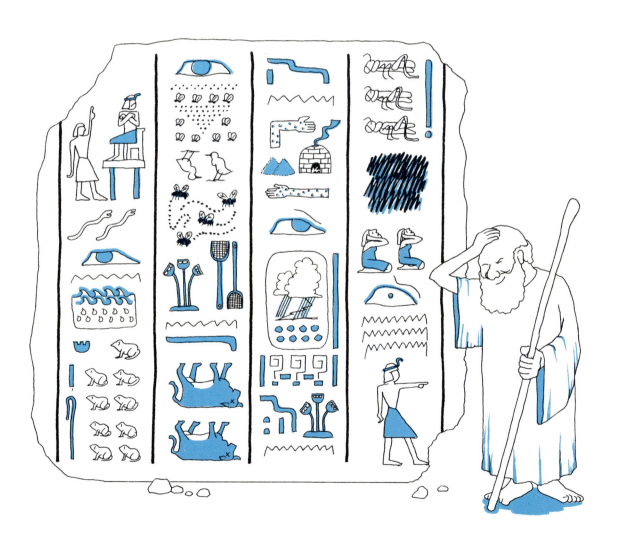

Then a terrible sickness came over Pharaoh and his people, and Pharaoh was really scared.

"Thus says the Lord," said Moses, "'Let my people go!'"

"Go," said Pharaoh. "Go!"

Off they went, free at last, the whole group of the Israelites, men and women and children, marching happily along until somebody looked back and said, "Oh, no!"

It turned out that Pharaoh had changed his mind again, and he was chasing after the Israelites, Pharaoh and all his troops. The Israelites walked faster and faster until they got to a large sea. There they were: the water in front of them and Pharaoh's armies behind them. They didn't know what to do.

"We're going to be slaves again," they said. "It's all over."

But it wasn't all over because God told Moses what to do again. Moses stretched his hand out over the sea, and the sea separated, right in the middle, and left a big dry path leading to the other side.

Moses and all the Israelites marched right down that path to the other side of the sea.

As soon as they got to the other side of the sea, they looked back and saw Pharaoh and his armies coming after them along the path in the middle of the sea. Then Moses stretched out his hand again, and the sea came rushing together right on top of Pharaoh and his troops. And to put it bluntly, they were drowned.

Which just goes to show that when God says God wants to set people free, God means it.

(Based on Exodus 3–14)

32

Rules

This is another story about a man named Moses. He was the chief of some people called the Children of Israel.

Once the Children of Israel were on a long journey, going through the wilderness to a place called the Promised Land.

You know what happens when you take a long trip with your brothers or sisters. You sit there in the back of the car, and for a while everything goes all right. You're friendly and you talk nicely and you enjoy the scenery. But after the trip has gone on a while, it all gets very BORING. And the more boring it gets, the easier it is to tease each other or nag each other or, sometimes, even hit each other.

That's what happened to the Children of Israel. They were taking this long trip, and the longer the trip got, the more bored they got. Before long they were teasing each other and nagging each other and beating up on each other and generally making a mess.

Moses, who was their chief, got tired of the mess. He did what people sometimes do when they get tired of messes; he went off by himself and prayed to God.

"God," he said, "what am I going to do with the Children of Israel? They're bored silly, and they're teasing each other, nagging each other, and beating up on each other. Something is missing."

"Rules!" said God.

"What?" asked Moses.

"Rules," said God. "That's what's missing. If the Children of Israel had some rules, they could get along much better with each other."

"All right," said Moses. "Can you give me some rules?"

"Of course," said God. "Here are a few. Don't worship any god but me. Honor your father and mother. Don't kill people or beat up on them. Don't steal. Don't lie."

Before God was through, God had given Moses ten rules, which Moses called the Ten Commandments.

When Moses had all Ten Commandments, he said to God, "Will the commandments which you have given to me make everything all right for the Children of Israel?"

"I wouldn't go that far," said God, "but they'll surely help."

"Well, then, God," said Moses. "Thank you very much."

(Based on Exodus 19:7–20:17)

Second Best

How was your day at school?" asked Mother.

"Lousy," said Tom, "just plain lousy."

"What went wrong?" asked his mother.

"Oh, I'm just so tired of being second best in everything," Tom answered. "Somebody can always beat me. I studied as hard as anybody else for the exam, and I still didn't do as well as Bob. I play as hard as anybody else at football, and I still didn't get chosen for the team. There's always somebody who's bigger than I am or smarter than I am or funnier than I am. I'm just not good for anything."

"Do you know who Samuel was?" asked his mother.

"Samuel who?"

"Just Samuel."

"Oh, that guy in the Bible."

"Yes. Well, one day God told Samuel that he wanted a new king for his people and that Samuel was supposed to go out and find the man. So Samuel went to Jesse. Jesse had nine sons, and God had told Samuel that one of Jesse's sons was supposed to be king.

"Samuel said to Jesse, 'I'm supposed to choose one of your sons to serve God as king. You'd better bring them out and show them to me.'

"Jesse brought out Eliab, the oldest, and said: 'Now this is my strongest son. Surely the Lord would like him to serve God and be king of Israel.'

"'No,' said Samuel, 'that's not the one.'

"So Jesse brought out Abinadab, the next oldest, and said, 'Now this is my smartest son. Surely the Lord would like him to serve God and be king of Israel.'

"'No,' said Samuel, 'that's not the one.'

"So Jesse brought out Shammah, the third son, and said, 'Now this is my friendliest son. Everybody likes him. Surely the Lord would like him to serve God and be king of Israel.'

"'No,' said Samuel, 'missed again.'

"So Jesse brought out his most musical son, and Samuel said, 'No.' Then Jesse brought out his most

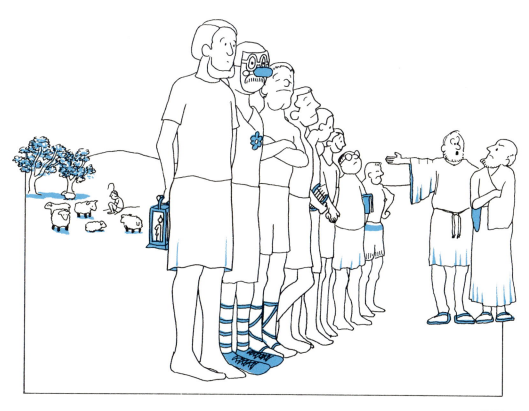

handsome son, and Samuel said, 'No.' So Jesse brought out his bravest son, and Samuel said, 'No.' So Jesse brought out his funniest son, and Samuel said, 'No.' So Jesse brought out his most honest son, and Samuel said, 'No, he's not the one either.'

"And Jesse said, 'That's it. I've run out of sons.'

"'Come on,' said Samuel. 'Isn't there anyone left?'

"'Well, there is the youngest one; he's out watching the sheep,' said Jesse. 'Frankly, I don't think he's up to being king of Israel and serving God.'

"'Let me see him,' said Samuel.

"So Jesse called in the youngest son, named David, from the field.

"'That's the one,' said Samuel. 'God wants to make him king.'

"'Now wait a minute,' said David. 'I'm not as strong as Eliab nor as smart as Abinadab nor as friendly as Shammah.'

"'I know,' said Samuel.

"'And I have a brother who is more musical than I and one who is handsomer and one who is braver and one who is funnier and one who is more honest.'

"'I know,' said Samuel.

"'You mean God loves me and wants me to serve him?' asked David.

"'Yes,' said Samuel. 'That's exactly what I mean.'"

Tom smiled at his mother. "You mean God loves me and wants me to serve him even though I'm not so good at everything?"

"Yes," said his mother. "That's exactly what I mean."

(Based on 1 Samuel 16:1-13)

38

Friends

Sometimes Bible stories tell us what we are supposed to do. "Do this or do that," they say, and we try our best to do this or do that. Sometimes Bible stories simply tell about the gifts which God has given us, the nice, special things which God has put in the world to make our lives good and special, too.

One of those gifts is friendship. This is a story about two friends and one king. The name of the king was Saul. He was not a wicked man, but he had a wicked temper. He spent lots of time yelling and throwing things around the palace, making quite a ruckus.

The king had a son named Jonathan. Jonathan was considerably quieter than his father and sometimes wished his father's temper wouldn't be so bad.

One day a young man came to the palace. His name was David. David and Jonathan liked each other immediately. They enjoyed the same games and the same food, and they sat up late at night talking to each other.

However, the king got angrier and angrier. He noticed that his son liked David better than he liked the king. Then the king noticed that EVERYONE liked David better than they liked the king.

So Saul spent more time than ever yelling and throwing things around the palace. Only now he threw things mostly in the direction of David.

40

At this point, David knew he was in trouble.

"I know I'm in trouble," said David to Jonathan. "Your father keeps throwing things. What should I do?"

"You go hide in the woods," said Jonathan. "When my father notices you're missing, we'll find out how angry he gets. If he *really* can't stand you, I'll warn you, and you can run away."

The first night the king noticed that David wasn't at dinner. "Where is that David?" asked the king. "He makes me so mad."

Jonathan heard him, but he didn't say anything.

The next night David wasn't at dinner again. *"Where is that David?"* asked the king. *"He makes me so mad."*

Then the king picked up a platter and threw it at Jonathan. Jonathan ducked and ran out to the field.

"David!" he cried.

David came out from the woods.

"David, David, run away before my father catches you. He's so angry he can hardly speak," Jonathan said.

"What will you do?" asked David.

"I'll stay here," said Jonathan. "I'll try to calm him down."

"But he may hurt you," said David.

"I'll stay here," said Jonathan. "I'll try to help. You run away."

David gave Jonathan a hug and ran as fast and as far as he could.

And many years later when he was very old and thought back on the nice gifts God had given him, he knew that one of the nicest was Jonathan who had been that special thing—his friend.

(Based on 1 Samuel 18:1–20:42)

41

Daniel, the King, and the Lions

Every country has a president or a governor or a king. Presidents, governors, and kings are very useful in helping people work together. When they are being good presidents, governors, or kings, they help keep people from hurting each other or going hungry or stealing from one another. So of course, presidents, governors, and kings are very important people.

But that doesn't mean that presidents, governors, and kings should think they can't do anything wrong. It doesn't mean that presidents and governors and kings should think that the job of people is to help *them,* because it's really the other way around. Their job is to help people.

Once in a while presidents, governors, and kings say to themselves: "I can do no wrong! I'll no longer serve the people of my country. The people of my country will serve me." We have a phrase for that. We say that when that happens, the president, governor, or king is "playing God." When presidents, governors, and kings play God, they make a BIG MISTAKE. Only God is allowed to play God.

That brings us to Daniel. He lived in a land where the king was named Darius, and Darius decided to play God in a big way. "You shall treat me as God," said Darius to the people. "You shall pray to me and bow before me, and you shall not pray to any other god or bow before any other god. If you do, I'll have you thrown into the lions' den." (The lions' den is where Darius kept his lions, who were not very friendly and *were* very hungry.)

Now Daniel was a faithful Jew; that means he knew there was only one God, and it certainly wasn't Darius. The only God was the Lord, while Darius (even though he dressed up and paraded a lot) was obviously only a man.

So while the other people in that country prayed to Darius and bowed down before Darius, Daniel knelt down three times a day and prayed to the Lord God.

The king had spies (kings who think they are God often hire spies to help them play God). The spies spied on Daniel as he was praying. They hurried to tell the king. "We caught Daniel praying to some God called the Lord," said the spies. "According to your own law you have to throw him into the lions' den."

"Oh, phooey!" said the king, for he really liked Daniel very much and didn't want him thrown into the lions' den. But he either had to stick by what he'd said or show that he wasn't always right; so he ended up doing what he hated doing. (This often happens to rulers who start playing God.)

The king had Daniel thrown into the lions' den. And he said (so no one else could hear), "God help you, Daniel!" And he meant it.

When Daniel landed in the lions' den, the lions got ready to prey, and Daniel got ready to pray. The lions licked their chops, and Daniel fell to his knees.

"Yum," said the lions, one to another.

"Help," said Daniel to God. "Give me courage, and then please get me out of this mess."

43

44

A remarkable thing happened. Daniel looked up from his prayers very cautiously, and he noticed that the lions had stopped drooling and started yawning. Then one by one the lions stretched out and went to sleep.

The next morning, King Darius came to the lions' den and cautiously opened the door. He hated to look inside; he was afraid the lions would be smiling happily, and Daniel would only be leftovers.

But Daniel was smiling happily, and the lions were snoring.

"Thank God," said King Darius.

"You said it," said Daniel.

Now, of course, this story doesn't mean that you should step inside the lions' cage at the local zoo. Daniel would have stayed outside the lions' den if he could have, and so should you. I wouldn't even suggest fooling around with fierce dogs or bothersome cats.

But when you are in a jam, you might remember that in the oddest ways and at the oddest times God gives courage and help to those who ask.

(Based on Daniel 6:6-24)

Running Away

Sometimes when people want us to understand something, they tell us a story. It doesn't really matter if the story is true just so long as we get the point.

One of the writers of the Bible wanted us to understand one thing: However much we may want to run away from God, we can't do it. God is always with us, and we can't escape God.

Now the Bible writer might just have written this sentence: "We can't run away from God." But then we might not have paid any attention to what God said.

Or the Bible writer might have written it in very large letters and underlined it: "WE CAN'T RUN AWAY FROM GOD." But the writer was afraid we still wouldn't remember. So instead, he told us a story.

Once there was a man named Jonah.

One day Jonah heard a voice:

"Jonah."

"Who's there?"

"The Lord."

"Oh," said Jonah. "What do you want?"

"I want you to go to Nineveh and preach a sermon for me."

"Thanks just the same," said Jonah, "but Nineveh is the last place I want to go."

The Lord didn't say anything more, so Jonah said to himself: "Who does the Lord think I am, anyway? God

46

has no right to tell me where to go. I'll just run away from God altogether. God said to go to Nineveh; I'll go to Tarshish."

So Jonah went to the nearest port and got on the first ship to Tarshish. And when he was on the ship, he sighed a sigh of relief. "Whew!" he said. "I'm free of the Lord at last." And he was so relieved that he fell asleep.

While Jonah was sleeping, the Lord sent a great storm; the ship was tossing up and down, and the sailors were all afraid.

And the captain came to Jonah and shook him and said, "Wake up, lazybones. There's a huge storm. Can you do anything about it?"

"Excuse me a minute," said Jonah. He went off into a corner of the ship and called softly, "Hey, Lord, are you still there?"

"Yes," said the Lord.

"I was afraid of that," said Jonah.

Then Jonah went back to the captain. "I'm sorry to say that this storm is all my fault," said Jonah. "You see, the Lord sent me to Nineveh, but I decided to run away to Tarshish instead. Now the Lord is mad at me. Maybe if I jump overboard, the Lord will save your ship."

So Jonah jumped overboard, and the storm ended; and before Jonah knew what was happening, a big fish swam up and swallowed him.

Jonah was inside the fish for three days and three nights, and he kept thinking to himself: "Well, I'm rid of the Lord at last. But I must say, I don't like it much without God. It's dark in here, and I'm awfully lonely."

Then Jonah thought, "Maybe I ought to pray. I doubt if the Lord will hear, but it's worth a try."

48

So Jonah began to pray: "Lord, it's dark and lonely inside this fish. Please help me."

He prayed like that for quite a while, and then he stopped and said: "Hey, Lord, by any chance, are you still there?"

And the Lord said, "Yes, Jonah, I'm still here."

"Glad to hear it," said Jonah. And just then the Lord made the fish spit Jonah out onto the dry land.

Jonah looked around, and he realized that he was right back where he'd started from. And then he heard a voice:

"Jonah."

"Who is it?"

"The Lord."

"You still there?" said Jonah.

"I'm always here," said the Lord.

"Oh," said Jonah. "What do you want?"

"I want you to go to Nineveh and preach a sermon for me."

"Right," said Jonah. "I'm on my way."

(Based on the Book of Jonah)

Timothy

There once was a bored and unhappy boy,
Whose life had no excitement or joy.
He said, "Nothing ever happens to me."
And the name of that boy was Timothy.

Timothy worked in his father's hotel,
Where he swept the floors or answered the bell
When somebody came to look for a room.
But he did his job with grump and gloom.

He said: "This job's as dull as it can be,
Since nothing ever happens to me.
I have a friend whose name is Mark,
Who sailed on a ship as big as the ark,
Across the wide and pounding sea;
But nothing ever happens to me."

"I have a friend whose name is Sam,
Who raised a small and woolly lamb
And won the prize at the village fair,
And people came from everywhere
To see that lamb. But golly, gee,
Nothing ever happens to me."

One night when Tim was sweeping the inn,
A man and a woman happened in;

50

51

Though the man looked tired and hungry, he smiled.
The woman—Tim saw—was expecting a child.
"What's your name?" asked the man.
                                        "Why, Timothy—

But nothing ever happens to me."

Then Timothy's father came to the door
And said, "We've got no room for more."
But the woman wept, and the man said, "Darn!"
So they found them a place to sleep in the barn.

Timothy swept the stable floor,
Thinking his life was just a bore.
Timothy made them a bed in the stall
And said: "I'm really sick of it all.
I'll go outside; there's nothing to see
Since nothing ever happens to me."

Timothy sat and moped until
He saw some shepherds come from the hill.
They said that angels had sung to them
Of what was happening in Bethlehem.
"An angel," said Tim, "is what I'd like to see,
But nothing ever happens to me."

Then came three kings from the distant East,
Riding on gangly and hump-backed beasts.
They told how they had followed a star
Across deserts and mountains to come this far.
"I wish I could travel," said Timothy,
"But nothing ever happens to me."

Then Timothy leaned against the door,
And never asked the reason for
The shepherds' and kings' going inside.
And he didn't peek in, or he might have spied
The shepherds bowing, the kings all kneeling
Before a baby. But Tim was feeling
Sad for himself. So he didn't say,
"What happened?" as they went away,
Or they might have told him a baby boy
Had been born that night to give us joy.
They might have said, as they laughed and smiled,
That God had sent Jesus, God's own dear child.

But all that Tim could think about
Was Timothy; so he quite missed out.
Because the world's biggest and best surprise
Had happened under his very eyes!
But he was just too grumpy to see,
Saying, "Nothing *ever* happens to me."

(Based on Matthew 2:1-12 and Luke 2:1-20)

53

Two Brothers

Once there were two brothers named James and John. Their father was a fisherman.

They used to talk about what they wanted to be when they grew up. "What do you want to be when you grow up?" asked James.

"A fisherman," said John. "What do you want to be when you grow up?"

"A fisherman," said James.

They went to their father and told him that they wanted to be fishermen. "First," said their father, "you must be big and strong. It takes big strong men to haul the nets full of fish."

So James and John ate well and slept well and exercised well and waited around for a long time until at last they were big and strong.

"Father," they said, "we're big and strong. Now can we be fishermen?"

"Not yet," said their father. "Next you have to learn how to fish. You have to learn where to cast the nets and how to haul the fish into the boat and how to mend the nets when they break."

So James and John studied and practiced until they learned where to cast the nets and how to haul the fish and how to mend the nets when they broke.

"Father," they said, "we've learned everything you told us to learn; now can we be fishermen?"

54

"Not yet," he said. "First you have to work for me long enough to make the money to buy your own boat."

"Oh," said James and John, a little disappointed. But they worked and they worked and they worked and at last they had earned enough to buy their own boat.

Then they went and bought a boat and rowed out onto the sea where their father was fishing. "Now," they said, "can we be fishermen?"

"Congratulations," said their father. "Now you are fishermen, indeed."

James and John loved their fishing. They were proud that they had waited long and worked hard to get everything they wanted.

But one day a strange thing happened to James and John. They had caught an especially large haul of fish. Some of the nets had broken, and they were sitting on the shore mending the nets.

Along came a man called Jesus. "James and John," he said, "I want you to leave everything and come work with me."

"You must be kidding," said James. "We spent all these years growing big and strong; then we studied and studied to learn how to fish; then we earned enough money to buy a boat. Do you want us to leave all that and work for you?"

"That's right," said Jesus.

James looked at John. John looked at James. They both looked at Jesus. They looked hard at Jesus.

Then they did something they couldn't quite believe. "All right," they said. And they left everything and followed him.

(Based on Mark 1:19-20)

Mark's Lunch

All through Mark's village the word spread quickly: "Jesus is coming! Jesus is coming here!"

Mark had heard a little about this Jesus, how he preached God's love and healed sick people and generally made quite an impression.

So Mark hurried home to tell his mother, "Jesus is coming to our town."

"So I hear," said his mother.

"Can I go see him?" asked Mark.

"You're pretty young to understand what's going on," said his mother. "I think maybe you'd better stay here."

"What if I can find someone to go with?" asked Mark.

"Then I suppose you can go," said his mother.

Mark ran to find his teacher. "Teacher," he said, "are you going to see Jesus?"

"Yes," said his teacher, "I thought I'd investigate to see what this Jesus is really like."

"Can I go with you?" asked Mark.

"I hardly think so," said the teacher. "This is really only a meeting for educated people who will understand what Jesus is trying to say."

"Oh," said Mark, quite disappointed. Then he ran to the synagogue to find his minister.

"Rabbi [which is what Jewish boys and girls call

their ministers], "are you going to see Jesus?"

"Well, I was a little curious about him," said the rabbi. "I thought I'd go."

"May I come with you?" asked Mark.

"I hardly think so," said the rabbi. "Jesus is concerned with very religious people and not with curious small boys."

"Oh," said Mark, very disappointed. He went home and moped around the kitchen till finally his mother

said, "Oh, all right, go see Jesus if you must. But be careful and don't stay too late." She packed Mark a lunch basket with bread and fish and sent him on his way.

When Mark got to the place where Jesus was preaching, a huge crowd was already gathered. Mark moved as far forward as he dared and stood behind his teacher and his minister, listening to Jesus talk.

When Jesus had talked a good long while, he realized that the people were getting hungry. "Who's got some food?" he asked.

"I do," said Mark.

"Hush," said his teacher.

"Shh!" said his minister.

"I do," said Mark a little louder.

"Come here," said Jesus.

Mark walked past the teacher and the minister, past all the big people sitting around Jesus.

He handed Jesus his lunch basket. "Here," he said.

"Thank you," said Jesus.

And then an amazing thing happened. Jesus took Mark's little lunch basket and out of it made enough food for everyone there to eat.

When Mark got home, his mother asked him, "What happened when you went to see Jesus?"

"You'd never believe it," said Mark. Then he went to bed.

(Based on John 6:1-13)

The Man Who Got Robbed

There once was a man who was going to Jericho.
He saddled his donkey and rode toward the town,
But robbers jumped out from the bushes and
  grabbed him,
Held him up, beat him up, then threw him down.

He lay in a ditch at the side of the highway.
He thought that he surely was going to die.
He feared that no one would know where to
  find him.
So he started to shout, and he started to cry:

  "Help! Help! Someone please help me!
  "Help! Help! Give me your aid.
  "Help! Help! Someone please help me!
  "I'm lying here wounded and weak and afraid."

Along came a minister on his way to a meeting.
He saw the man lying there, heard the man cry.
He said, "I'm too busy," and crossed to the other
Side of the road, then looked down and passed by.

The man in the ditch was sad and discouraged.
Would no one come by who would help him at all?
Then he heard footsteps, and someone was singing.
He gathered his strength, and he started to call:

60

"Help! Help! Someone please help me!
"Help! Help! Give me your aid.
"Help! Help! Someone please help me!
"I'm lying here wounded and weak and afraid."

Along came an organist, humming and singing.
He hummed all the louder, the more the man cried.
He tried not to look at the man in the ditch,
But he hurried and scurried on the other side.

The man in the ditch grew sadder and sadder.
Would nobody help him? Were all filled with fear,
Or too busy, or selfish? Then he decided
To cry out once more as some hoof-steps drew near.

"Help! Help! Someone please help me!
"Help! Help! Give me your aid.
"Help! Help! Someone please help me!
"I'm lying here wounded and weak and afraid."

Then down the road there rode a Samaritan.
The man in the ditch was sure he was through
Since he and his friends didn't like the Samaritans.
This man would ignore him—what could he do?

But what a surprise! The Samaritan stopped,
Got off the donkey, knelt down by the man,
Gave him some medicine, gave him some bandages,
Said, "I'll do as much as I possibly can."

The Samaritan led the poor man to an inn;
He said to the innkeeper, "Give him a bed.
Feed him and give him whatever he needs,
But don't give him the bill; I'll pay it instead."

And that is the end of this very old story.
It ends as a very old story should end.
The man in the ditch was amazed to discover,
When he least expected it, the love of a friend.

(Based on Luke 10:25-37)

Lucy and the Shepherd

It was bedtime, and Mother had already told her a story, but still Lucy couldn't sleep.

"Mommy," she asked, "do you love me?"

"Yes, Lucy."

"And does Daddy?"

"Yes, Lucy."

"And does God love me?"

"Yes, Lucy."

"How much?"

"How much what?"

"How much does God love me?"

"Very much."

"How much is very much?"

"A lot."

"Oh."

"Goodnight, Lucy."

"Goodnight, Mommy."

"Mommy. . . ."

"Yes, Lucy?"

"How much is a lot?"

"What?"

"You said God loves me a lot. How much is a lot?"

"Well, once Jesus said that God is like a shepherd. You know what a shepherd is?"

"A man who takes care of sheep."

"Yes, and Jesus told a story about a shepherd. One

day one of the shepherd's sheep got lost. The shepherd left all the other sheep behind, and he walked along the mountainside looking everywhere for the lost sheep. The night got darker, and the wind got colder, and the shepherd kept on looking just the same. After a long time he came to the steepest side of the mountain. He leaned over the steep cliff, and he saw the lost sheep caught in a bush. So the shepherd started slowly, carefully, down the cliff. He scratched his arms, and he scraped his legs. He very nearly fell. But at last he came to the place where the sheep was. He lifted the lost sheep in his arms and brought it all the way back to the pasture, carrying it all the way back to the flock. And only then did he put it down."

"Gosh," said Lucy. "The shepherd loved that sheep a lot."

"Yes," said Lucy's mother, "he did."

"Then," said Lucy, "is that how much God loves me?"

"Yes," said her mother. "That much and more."

(Based on Luke 15:1-7)

The Good Father

Once Jesus told a story about how much God loves and forgives us. He said that God is like a certain father.

This father had two sons, and one day his youngest son came up to him and said, "Father, I want my allowance."

"Well, it isn't quite time for your allowance," said the father, "but I guess that can be arranged."

"No," said the son, "you don't understand. I don't just want this week's allowance. I want all the allowance you're going to pay me for all the years ahead."

"Right now?" asked the father.

"Yes, please," said the son.

It wasn't easy for the father to scrape together all the money which the son wanted, but he managed to do it. He gave the money to the son, and the son said, "Thank you very much. Now I'm leaving home."

"What?" asked the father.

"I'm leaving home. I want to try life on my own. Good-bye."

The son packed up his baggage, and he took his money, and he left home. He walked, and he walked, and he walked, and he walked. Finally he came to a place called the Far Country.

He liked the Far Country because it was so different from home. There were bright lights and pretty women, all dressed up. And best of all, there were all kinds of interesting things you could spend your money on.

The son tried all the things you could spend your money on. He woke up one morning and discovered that all his money was gone. He had wasted it all.

"What will I do?" he wondered. It so happened that the Far Country had a number of pig farms in it, and the son went to one of the pig farmers.

"May I help you raise pigs?" he asked.

"It's dirty business," said the farmer, "but if you want to, you may."

So the son took the bucket full of pig food, and he went out to the pigsty and began to feed the pigs.

Suddenly he realized something. "These pigs eat better than I do," he said. "I've really made a mess of my life. What will I do?"

He thought, and he thought, and at last he had an idea. "I'll go back to my father's house," he said. "Maybe my father will let me be a worker on his farm. At least that way I'll have enough to eat."

So the son left the pig farm, and he walked, and he walked, and he walked, and he walked until he had left the Far Country far behind. As he came to his own country, he began to get nervous. "I'll bet my father will really be angry with me," he thought. "After all, I took all the money and spent it."

As he neared his own house, the son thought, "Boy, maybe this isn't such a good idea. Maybe I'll really be in trouble."

As he came to his own street, the son thought, "I wonder what Father. . . ."

But before he could wonder any more, he saw his father run down the steps of the house and down the walk and onto the street, and down the street to greet him.

The son started to say, "Father, I'm. . . ." But before he could finish the sentence, his father threw his arms around him and hugged him and kissed him and welcomed him home.

(Based on Luke 15:11-24)

Gratitude

When John sat down at the dinner table, he was starving. His mother had made hamburgers, his favorite food, and John immediately began to wolf down the hamburger that was on his plate.

"Wait a minute," said John's father. "Aren't you forgetting something?"

"What?" asked John.

"Aren't you forgetting that we give thanks for food, for the good gifts God gives us?"

"Why do we have to give thanks?" asked John. "I'm too hungry to give thanks."

"We're going to say grace," said John's father. "And after we've said grace, I'll tell you a story."

"Oh, all right."

The family said grace, and then as John started to eat his hamburger, John's father started to tell the story:

Once upon a time there were ten men who had a very strange disease. Their names were Abner and Bertrand and Caspar and Douglas and Evan and Frederick and George and Hiram and Ian and John. Because people were scared of this strange disease, everyone stayed away from them; so the ten sick men always hung around with each other.

One day Abner came home and told Bertrand and Caspar and Douglas and Evan and Frederick and

George and Hiram and Ian and John that he had some very good news. "Jesus is coming to our town!" he said. "Jesus may be able to heal our strange disease."

The ten sick men went to the center of town. As soon as they saw the ten sick men, all the other people in the town ran away. So the sick men were standing there at the center of town all by themselves.

Pretty soon along came Jesus. And Abner and Bertrand and Caspar and Douglas and Evan and Frederick and George and Hiram and Ian and John all cried out with one voice: "Jesus, Master, have mercy on us."

And Jesus *did* have mercy on them. Jesus reached out and healed Abner, and Abner was so excited that he ran right home to all his friends. Jesus healed Bertrand, and Bertrand was so excited that he ran right home to tell all his friends. Jesus healed Caspar, and Caspar ran home to tell all his friends. Jesus healed Douglas, who ran home to tell all his friends; and Evan, who ran home to tell all his friends; and Frederick, who ran home to tell all his friends; and George, who ran home to tell all his friends; and Hiram, who ran home to tell all his friends; and Ian, who ran home to tell all his friends, and John, who ran home—well, *almost* ran home. . . .

Because before he got to his house, John suddenly remembered something very important! And he turned around and ran back to Jesus; he knelt down at Jesus' feet and said, "Thank you, Lord, for your kindness. Thank you for the gift of healing you have given me."

"Thank you, John," said Jesus. "All ten of you had your bodies made well, but only you had your heart made well, too."

(Based on Luke 17:11-19)

71

Zacchaeus

Once there was a man named Zacchaeus. You need to know two things about Zacchaeus.

The first thing you need to know is that Zacchaeus was very short. He was so short that he couldn't look other people in the eye. He always looked them in the stomach. He was so short that other people often didn't notice him; so his foot was often stepped on by someone else's foot. His head was often elbowed by someone else's elbow. "I hate being short," said Zacchaeus to himself. But he *was* short; so what could he do?

The other thing you need to know about Zacchaeus is that he was a tax collector. You may have heard your mother or father talk about taxes. Probably they don't like taxes very much. Taxes are payments people make to the government. They have to be paid, but no one much likes paying them. And unfortunately, most people don't much like the people who collect the payments. That is, most people don't much like tax collectors.

When Zacchaeus walked along the street, if people noticed him at all, they said, "Hiss! Boo! Here comes the tax collector." When Zacchaeus invited people to his house for dinner, they always said, "Sorry, we're busy."

"I hate being a tax collector," said Zacchaeus to himself. But he liked the money which came with his job; so what could he do?

One day Zacchaeus, the short tax collector, heard that Jesus was coming to his town. Zacchaeus had heard that Jesus loved all sorts of people; so Zacchaeus thought to himself, "Maybe Jesus will like me. If I invite Jesus to dinner, maybe *he* will come."

Zacchaeus hurried to the town gate where Jesus was to arrive. There was a huge crowd of people gathered around the gate, wanting to see Jesus. The crowd was full of people who were much taller than Zacchaeus; so that he couldn't even see the road where Jesus would be walking.

Zacchaeus tried to push ahead to his left, but his foot was stepped on by someone's shoe. "Ouch!" said Zacchaeus.

"Who's down there?" asked a voice.

"It's me, Zacchaeus."

"Hiss! Boo!" said the voice.

Zacchaeus tried to push ahead to his right, but an elbow elbowed him in the head. "Ouch!" said Zacchaeus.

"Who is that?" asked a voice.

"It's me, Zacchaeus."

"Hiss! Boo!" said the voice.

Zacchaeus tried to push his way straight ahead, but the crowd pushed him straight back. He pushed harder, and the crowd pushed harder. Zacchaeus felt a thud as he hit his head against a tree.

He put his hand on his sore head, and then he had an idea. "I'll climb the tree," he said. "Then I can see Jesus. Then Jesus can see me."

So Zacchaeus shinnied up the tree till he got to the very top.

The branches rustled under his weight. The crowd looked up. "Who's there?" they shouted.

"It's me, Zacchaeus."

"Hiss! Boo!" said the crowd.

"What are you doing up in that tree?" someone asked.

"I'm going to see Jesus," said Zacchaeus. "I'm going to ask him to have dinner with me."

"You!" said a voice. "No one wants to have dinner with you. You know what he'll say—'Sorry, I'm busy'—that's what he'll say."

Just then Jesus came to the city gate. He passed through the gate and walked along the road. He walked along the road and stopped by the tree. He looked up into the tree and smiled.

"Zacchaeus," he said. "Hurry up and scoot down

74

from that tree. I want to have dinner at your house tonight."

So Zacchaeus shinnied down the tree and took Jesus home and the two of them ate together with much joy.

(Based on Luke 19:1-10)

The Son of God

The news spread all through Jerusalem: "The Son of God is coming. The Son of God is coming tomorrow!"

As soon as Simon heard, he rushed home to tell his mother. "Mother, the Son of God is coming tomorrow; may we go see him?"

"Of course, my son," his mother said.

That night Simon was so excited that he couldn't sleep. What would the Son of God look like? Simon had seen the son of the governor once; he had come riding through the streets in a chariot with prancing horses, while drums were beating, and trumpets were sounding, and soldiers were marching by his side. And Simon had seen the son of the king; he had walked through the streets in rich robes, surrounded by friends who listened carefully to every word he said and laughed loudly at each joke he made. But Simon had never seen the Son of God. What a wonderful thing: to be the Son of God! Surely the Son of God would come in a chariot more splendid than the chariot of the governor's son, with louder drums and louder trumpets and ten times as many soldiers marching by his side. Surely he would be dressed more finely than the king's son, surrounded by more talking, laughing friends. Simon could hardly wait to see him.

When morning came at last, Simon took his mother

by the hand, and they walked to the street by the city gate, where the Son of God was to enter Jerusalem. Before long they heard the shouts of the people: "Hosanna! Hosanna!" Simon looked eagerly for the sight of a chariot or a man in rich robes surrounded by friends; he listened eagerly for the sound of drums and trumpets and laughter. The shouts grew louder and louder; people began pressing forward and breaking loose from the crowd, taking palm branches and throwing them into the road. "Hosanna! Hosanna!" At last a huge cheer burst from the crowd: "It is the Son of

God!" But what Simon saw was not a governor's son in a great chariot with drums and trumpets and marching soldiers, nor a king's son in rich robes surrounded by laughing friends: what Simon saw was a poor, tired, dusty man, riding on a poor, tired, dusty donkey through the midst of the cheering crowds.

"Is that the Son of God?" asked Simon.

"Yes, my son," his mother said.

"But he looks so poor and tired," said Simon.

"Yes, my son," his mother said.

Simon looked hard at the man; he thought a minute.

"And something else," said Simon.

"What's that?" asked his mother.

"He looks so very lonely," Simon said.

"Yes, my son," his mother said.

Later, as they were walking home, Simon had to ask his mother about what they had seen.

"Mother, isn't it strange that the Son of God should be a poor man on a donkey?"

"Yes, my son, it is very strange."

Simon was quiet for a few minutes, then, "Mother?"

"Yes, my son?"

"Isn't it strange that the Son of God should look so lonely?"

"Yes, my son, it's very strange."

"Mother?"

"Yes?"

"And kind of wonderful?" asked Simon.

"Yes, my son, and very wonderful, indeed."

(Based on Mark 11:1-10)

78

A Trip to the Temple

It was Passover, the great holiday of the Jewish people. Matthew and his mother and father had traveled many, many miles from Egypt to Jerusalem. They wanted to visit the great temple of the Jewish people which was in Jerusalem. They wanted to celebrate the holiday there in the holiest building in the world.

For many months Matthew had saved money so that he could make an offering at the temple. He had run errands for his mother and done odd jobs around his neighborhood. Now he had saved five dollars. It was more money than he had ever owned in his life, and he could hardly wait to bring it to the temple and make an offering to God.

When Matthew and his parents arrived at the temple after their long journey, they were amazed at how many people were pushing their way into the holy building. Jewish people from all over the world had come together to celebrate the Passover. It was exciting and a little frightening to see all those people—they were speaking different languages and pushing and shoving a bit to get in the temple gates.

Also Matthew noticed that there were shops inside the courtyard of the temple. He thought it a little odd that people would be selling things inside the temple itself, but he was too excited to pay much attention.

He went with his father and mother through the

courtyard and in the doors of the inner temple. He started to go to the table where people collected the offerings for God's work. He reached into his pocket, and he took out the five dollars he had worked so hard to earn. He was going to give this money to God.

But just as Matthew reached out to put his money in the offering box, a man reached out to stop him.

"I'm sorry, Son," said the man, "but that money won't do."

Matthew didn't understand. "I earned this money," he said. "I brought it as my offering to God."

"Yes," said the man, "that's all very well and good. But this is Egyptian money. The rule is that you have to put money from this country in the offering box."

"Where can I get the right kind of money?" asked Matthew.

"Fortunately," said the man, "there's a little bank right out there in the courtyard you just came through. You take your five Egyptian dollars to the banker, and he'll give you the right kind of money."

Matthew looked at his father in bewilderment. "I didn't know God was so fussy about what kind of money we give him," said Matthew.

"God *isn't,*" said his father. "But these people are. Come on, we might as well exchange your money."

Matthew and his parents went to the bank in a corner of the courtyard. A banker sat behind a table collecting money from foreign countries and trading it for local money.

Matthew gave the man his five dollars. "Please, sir," he said, "I want to exchange this for money I can use to make an offering to God."

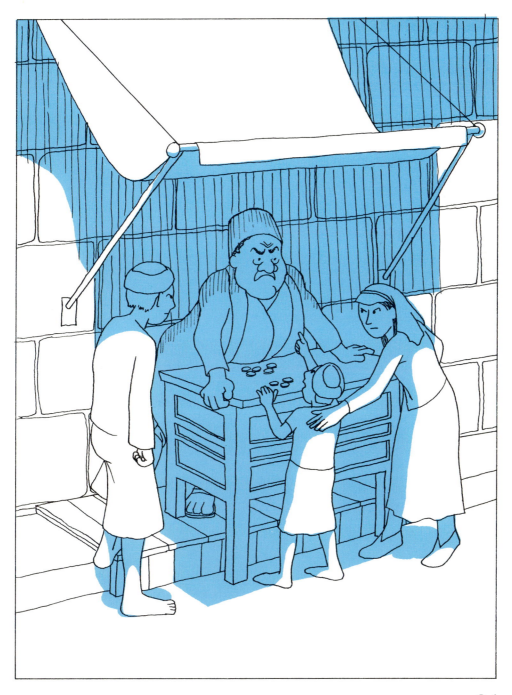

"Fine, fine," said the man. He took the five dollars and put it in his pile of Egyptian money. Then he reached into the box where he kept temple money. He counted out three dollars and handed them to Matthew.

"Wait a minute!" said Matthew. "I gave you five dollars, and you gave me only three in return. That's not fair."

"Fair," said the man, "fair? This is the real world, Sonny. You don't think I'm going to change your money without making a little for myself!"

"You didn't just make a little," said Matthew's mother. Matthew's father hushed her and moved them both quickly away.

"It's not fair, Father," cried Matthew. "It's not fair."

"I know, Son."

"What can we do about it?"

"There's not much we can do about it," said Matthew's father. "If we make trouble, we'll get in trouble. The temple leaders are stronger than we. All we can do is pray that some day God will make the temple good and holy again."

Matthew was very sad as he took his three dollars to the offering box. Somehow the joy had gone out of his giving. He wanted to give five dollars to God's work, not three dollars to God and two dollars to the banker. As he put his money in the box, he whispered a prayer: "Please, God, do something. Do something to make the temple good and holy again. These people are ruining your house."

When Matthew and his parents came out of the inner rooms of the temple into the courtyard, they heard a terrible commotion. People were yelling and screaming; birds which had been carefully caged were fluttering and flying away from the temple yard.

On the other side of the temple, at the center of the noise, Matthew saw a strong young man with a whip. The young man was whipping the birdcages off their stands; the cages were breaking, and the birds were flying away.

Then the young man ran up to the bank where Matthew had exchanged his money. He put down his whip. He took the banking table in his two hands, and he tipped it over. The banker fell back in dismay. The young man took the banker's money and scattered it on the temple floor.

"This is God's house, a place for prayer. You have made it a house for thieves!" the young man said.

Then the young man called to some friends. Together they ran quickly from the temple courtyard and disappeared.

The bankers were busily trying to gather their money, and the bird-sellers were desperately chasing after the few birds they could find.

Some of the people were laughing. "Ha, good for Jesus," they said. "He told them off; he really did."

Matthew's father turned to Matthew's mother. "I don't understand," he said. "What did all that mean?"

But Matthew only smiled to himself. He knew what it meant. God had heard Matthew's prayer. God had sent someone to make the temple good and holy again.

(Based on Mark 11:15-18)

Martha's Hero, I

Martha had a hero. She had first seen him from a great distance, standing on a mountainside surrounded by people. Though she was a long way off and couldn't always understand what he was saying, she liked the sound of his voice, the strength of his smile.

The next time her hero came to town, Martha thought she'd get a little closer; so she nudged herself up as close as she dared, standing just behind her hero's closest friends, listening to what he said. Occasionally she peeked around the big person in front of her and looked at her hero's face; she loved his smile. She wished she might get closer. You'd almost think her hero had heard Martha's wish. The next time she peeked around the big person in front of her, her hero stopped what he was saying.

"Hey, big people," he said, "why don't you get out of the way and let the children come up here in front? Remember that God's kingdom belongs to them."

Martha didn't know exactly what that meant, but she did know that she was thrilled to be sitting so close to her hero. Once he even reached out and touched her shoulder as he told a story to the people sitting around.

Now Martha had a secret collection of special treasures. She had a piece of ribbon from her birthday party. She had a beautiful stone from the bottom of the stream near her house. She had a bird's nest she had found where it had fallen from a tree. More than anything else Martha wanted something to treasure from her hero.

The next time Martha's hero came to town, she decided to be very brave, though she was afraid to be very brave as well.

Martha went right down to the town square where her hero was helping some sick people get well. She waited until there was a break between healings, and she edged up beside him. "Sir," she said quietly. Unfortunately, lots of other people were trying to get his attention, too.

"JESUS," said Martha more loudly. Her hero turned around. Martha was embarrassed by the loudness of her own voice. "Sir," she said again very softly, "I wonder if I could have some little souvenir from you to put in my box of treasures."

Jesus smiled. He reached into the bag he carried, and he brought forth a very small scroll with some special words about God written on the scroll. "Why don't you keep this in your box of treasures?" said Jesus.

"Oh, thank you," said Martha. She ran home and hid the little scroll away in her treasure box.

Several days later, Martha came home from school. She came into the living room and saw a terrible thing. Martha's little brother had found her treasure box. He had spilled the treasures all over the floor. The ribbon was dirty; the stone had disappeared; the bird's nest was scattered in twigs and pieces. Worst of all, Martha's little brother had torn her scroll in two. The sad pieces lay on the floor.

Martha was outraged. Tears came to her eyes. "I'll never forgive you," she said to her brother. "Never."

Martha ran crying out of her house and ran and ran as far as she could go. "How could he do that?" she thought. "I can't stand that little brat."

When Martha had gone as far as she could go, she found that she had come to a part of town she didn't recognize. There was a large hill, and people were climbing slowly up the hill, as if something exciting was there to be seen. Martha couldn't stand the thought of going home and seeing that stupid brother of hers; so she followed the people up the long hill to see what she could see.

She didn't like what she saw. She had heard about such things, but she had never seen them: crucifixions. Three men were hanging on wooden crosses with nails in their hands and feet. They were dying. The Romans were killing them.

Martha was terrified. She didn't want to look, and yet somehow she wasn't ready to leave. Finally she looked up. She couldn't believe what she saw. On the middle cross hung her hero, Jesus, nails in his hands and nails in his feet. They were killing him. Those Romans were killing him.

Martha couldn't believe it. "How could they do that?" she thought. "I can't stand them."

She couldn't run away. That was her hero there, and she couldn't leave. She moved as close as she could to the cross. She wanted to cry out, to say something, but she couldn't think what to say. So she just stood there.

Around her were the soldiers, the awful men who had hurt and broken the man she loved.

Finally Jesus said something. "Father God," he said. "Forgive these people for killing me. They don't know what they're doing."

Martha turned and ran down the hill. Tears were running down her face, and her heart felt as though it would choke. She ran and ran and ran until she came to her own house. She opened the door, and there was her brother sitting on the floor, dirty and bratty as ever.

Martha didn't know what to say; so finally she just sat down beside him. "Hello," she said. "I'm home."

(Based on Luke 23:32-38)

Martha's Hero, II

"Martha," called her father, "come to dinner."

"No," cried Martha. "I don't feel like it."

"Martha, Martha," said her mother. "This is the most important holiday of the year. We're having a special meal. Now, you come."

"I don't care," said Martha, "I'm not coming."

Martha's father came into her room.

"Martha, what's the matter?"

"They killed him; they killed Jesus. I can't believe it. What harm did he ever do to anyone?"

"I'm sorry, Martha," said her father. "That's very sad and very unfair, but we need to keep going even when terrible things happen."

"I don't want to keep going," said Martha. "I just want to be left alone."

"Martha," said her father. "This is the Passover. This is the night when we remember how God took the people of Israel out of Egypt where they were slaves and led them to the Promised Land."

"I don't feel like it," said Martha. "Do I have to come eat?"

"Yes," said her father. "Maybe you'll feel better soon."

Martha sat at the table, and she barely listened as her father talked about the time when God led the Children of Israel out of Egypt into the Promised Land.

To be sure, God had saved God's people from slavery. But Jesus had loved God; Jesus had loved God more than anyone Martha had ever seen. Why didn't God do something for Jesus? Why didn't God save him, too?

At last the meal was ending. Martha's father prayed a prayer which somehow stuck in her mind: "Almighty God, you turn our deepest sorrow into greatest joy."

"Our deepest sorrow into greatest joy"—all Martha could feel was the sorrow. How could Jesus be dead? Why did they kill him? It wasn't fair.

All the next day she barely felt like doing anything. She ate her meals slowly and sadly. She didn't pay much attention to her parents or her little brother. She could hardly wait until dark when she could sleep and try to forget.

At last the darkness came. Martha lay down on the pallet where she slept and dozed badly through the long dull night.

Suddenly, out of her light sleep she heard excited voices in the other room. She crept quietly in. Her mother was talking to her father, talking quietly but very excitedly.

"Martha," said her mother, looking up. "We've just heard. We've just got the news. God has raised Jesus from the dead. Jesus is dead no longer. He lives forever—forever."

Martha didn't know what to say. With tears in her eyes she turned and went back to her own room. She knelt on the floor in the gathering dawn, and she quietly prayed: "Almighty God, you turn our deepest sorrow into greatest joy."

(Based on Luke 23:55—24:9)

The Man Who Didn't Like Anything New

Once there was a man who didn't like anything new. The man's name was Paul.

Paul always wore a brown robe with brown sandals. One day a friend of his said, "Paul, why don't you buy a blue robe and black sandals?" Paul said, "Absolutely not. I don't like anything new."

Every Tuesday and Thursday night Paul's mother fixed fish for dinner. One Tuesday night Paul came home and discovered that his mother had fixed lamb instead. "Oh, Mother," he complained, "you know I don't like anything new."

Paul was a very religious person. He loved to go to synagogue (which was his church). He went every Friday night and every Saturday. One time the rabbi (the name for his minister) introduced a new prayer into the service. Paul was very upset. "Rabbi, Rabbi," he said. "You know I don't like anything new."

One day one of Paul's friends came to visit him in Paul's shop. "Hello, Paul," said the friend. "What's new?"

"Nothing, thank heaven," said Paul "What's new with you?"

"You'll never guess, " said Paul's friend. *"God* has done something new."

"God!" said Paul. "First my friend tries to get me to buy a blue robe. Then my mother tries to get me to eat lamb on Tuesday. Then the rabbi says a new prayer.

91

Now you tell me that even God is doing something new!"

"That's right," said Paul's friend. "God has sent God's Son, Jesus. And even though people killed Jesus, God made him alive again. Now Jesus lives in the hearts of people who believe in him."

"No!" said Paul. "I won't believe it. I refuse to believe that God would do anything new. I don't like this Jesus, and I don't like the people who follow him."

Paul was so angry that he went to the police chief. "There are some dangerous people running around," said Paul. "They say that God has done something new

and sent a man named Jesus. I want to arrest them."

"Good idea," said the chief of police, and then and there he made Paul a deputy. "Go get them," he said.

Paul got on his horse and rode off to arrest the people who followed Jesus. He was riding hard and fast, thinking to himself, "I'll get them!"

Suddenly there was a blinding light as though all the lightning in the world had been rolled together and then unwound in one great FLASH. Paul fell off his horse and covered his eyes. Then Paul heard a voice:

"Paul! Why are you arresting the people who love me?"

"Who is it?" asked Paul.

"It's me, Jesus," said the voice.

"I was afraid of that," said Paul. "What do you want?"

"I want you to stop hurting me and start helping me," said Jesus. "I want you to tell everyone that God has done something new, that God really did send me to show God's love."

"All right," said Paul, "you win."

Paul, still blinded by the light, got on his horse.

As he rode along, he thought more and more about the voice, about Jesus, about himself.

Finally, Paul arrived home. He went into his house and sat down at the table. "Hello, Paul," said his mother. "What's new?"

"I am," said Paul. "*I* am."

(Based on Acts 9:1-19)

Index of Scripture Passages